Table of C

Introduction

Do you think you know your mom? You'd probably answer, Yes! But think again, she spent many precious years in your upbringing which you won't remember a lot about. You would be surprised to know how much time and effort she has invested in it. There have been innumerable sleepless nights and moments, you'll only experience when you're a parent yourself. Although you can never pay back what your mother has always done for you, the least you can do is regard her. It's about time that you get to know her story and acknowledge her unconditional love, unquestionable devotion and selflessness.

Useful tips

There are no strict rules for the way you use the book.

Although you may need to keep somethings in mind:

- Fill this book with memories from your heart, there's no need to be complex or formal.
- Keep in mind that this book isn't meant to put you in a corner, it's meant to pass love. So don't enter information you don't want to be passed on to your children.
- There's no correct way of filling in this book. You can start from wherever you like and fill in any order.
- This book has 4 chapters, Fatherhood, Childhood, Teenage, and Adulthood. It's totally up to you to decide which ones to complete first.
- Filling this book in one session is not recommended as there are a lot of questions. Multiple sessions would be suitable; however, you may choose as comfortable.
- If you find that some questions are irrelevant, unsuitable, or you are not comfortable in answering them for any reasons, feel free to skip them.
- If you find that something important was missed out, write it in the "Additional Notes" pages which are given at the end of each section.
- If you don't have any additional notes, you can utilize the space by pasting some memorable photos.

Family Tree

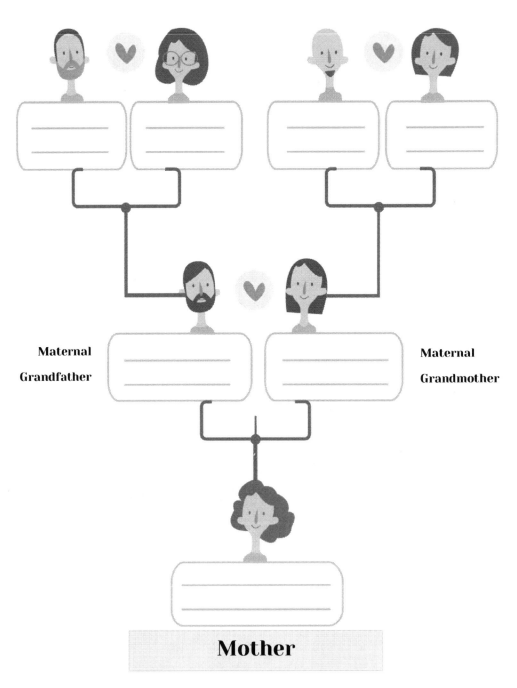

Great Grandparents   Great Grandparents

Maternal
Grandfather

Maternal
Grandmother

Mother

Mom's Life Timeline

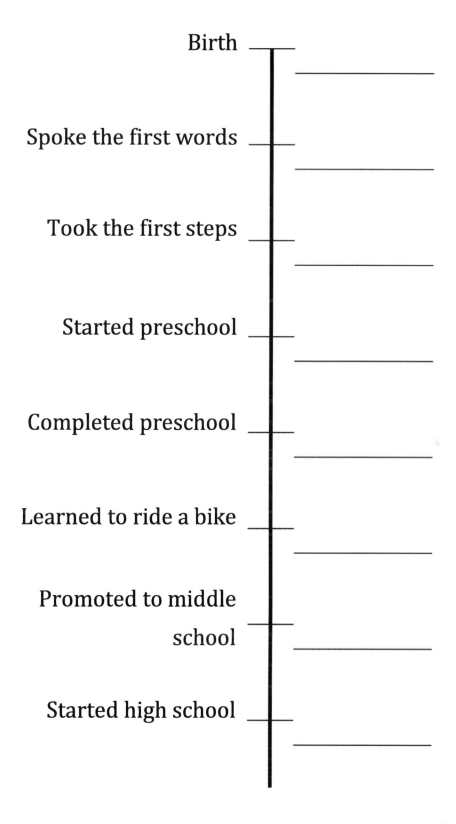

Birth

Spoke the first words

Took the first steps

Started preschool

Completed preschool

Learned to ride a bike

Promoted to middle school

Started high school

Went to college

Drove a car for the first time

Completed college

Started university

Graduated

Got the first job

Got the first paycheck

5

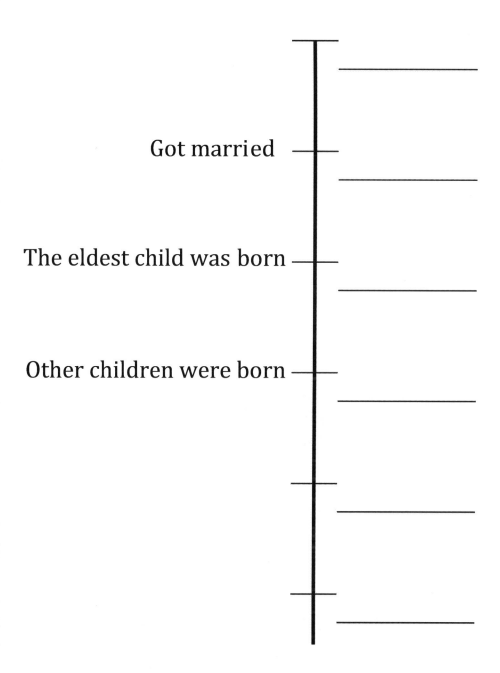

Got married

The eldest child was born

Other children were born

Childhood

"Childhood is the one story that stands by itself in every soul."

— Ivan Doig

1) What is your birth date?

_____

2) What is your full name? Who named you at birth?

_____

_____

3) What does your name mean?

_____

_____

4) Do you like your name? If not, would you change it? What would

you change it to?

_____

5) Were you named after someone? If so, who was it?

_____

6) Did you have a nickname? Who gave it to you?

_____

7) Where were you born and in which city?

_____

8) How old were your parents when you were born?

_____

9) Were you the eldest, middle, or youngest child?

_____

10) How many siblings did you have and what is your age difference with them?

_____

_____

11) Are there any stories in your family about you as a baby?

_____

_____

_____

12) What did your parents tell you about how you looked as an infant?

_____

_____

13) Did you have a resemblance with your parents or some other relative?

_____

14) What were your first words?

_____

_____

15) What is your earliest childhood memory?

_____

_____

_____

16) Did you belong to a wealthy, middle class or low income household? How did you feel about it?

_____

_____

_____

17) What was your parents' occupation in your childhood?

_____

_____

18) Do you remember where they worked? Did you ever visit their workplace?

_____

_____

19) What do you admire most about your father?

_____

_____

_____

20) What do you admire about your mother?

_____

_____

_____

21) What hobbies or interests did your parents have in your childhood?

_____

_____

22) What was the first book that you ever read?

_____

_____

23) Did you receive an allowance? How much? How did you spend it?

_____

_____

24) Did your family follow any religious traditions? If so, do you continue to follow them?

_____

_____

_____

25) Which characteristics of each of your parents stood out the most?

_____

_____

_____

_____

26) Were your parents strict? What rules did they make you follow?

_____

_____

_____

27) How was your relationship with your siblings?

_____

_____

28) What language(s) were spoken by your parents?

_____

_____

29) Did you have a bike? How much did you enjoy riding it?

_____

_____

30) Did you prefer indoor games, outdoor, or both?

_____

_____

31) What were your favorite activities and hobbies? What games did you like to play?

_____

_____

32) Did you like to do them alone or with someone else?

_____

33) As a child, whose presence made you feel:

Happy:

_____

Angry:

_____

Secure:

_____

Uncomfortable:

_____

Afraid:

_____

34) Did you have a pet? If so, what did you call it and how long did it stay with you?

_____

_____

35) What was your most prized possession as a kid?

_____

_____

_____

36) What was your favorite costume you ever wore?

_____

_____

37) Did your family have any traditions? Describe them.

_____

_____

_____

38) Share a few memories of your home?

_____

_____

_____

39) What can you recall about your room?

_____

_____

_____

40) Did you have to share it with someone or had it all to yourself?

41) As a child, what were your greatest fears?

42) What was the most embarrassing thing you did as a kid?

43) Which meals did you grow up eating regularly?

44) What do you miss the most from your childhood?

45) Is there anything you really wanted to talk to your parents about, but never did?

_____

_____

_____

46) How do you think you are similar to and different from your parents?

_____

_____

_____

47) How do you think you have made your parents proud?

_____

_____

48) When you were a kid, what did you want to be? Why?

_____

_____

49) Who was your role model and how did you try to become like them?

50) Do you think your 10-year-old self would be proud of your present self?

51) What did you have as a child that a kid in the present will not have?

52) Were you more attached to your mother or father? Why?

53) What did you really wanted to know about your parents, but never did?

_____

_____

54) Did you travel abroad with your family? Where did you go and how was the experience?

_____

_____

55) At what age did you start school and where?

_____

_____

56) Who was your "best friend"?

_____

57) Who were your other close friends?

_____

_____

58) Who were your first friends at school and in the neighborhood?

_____

_____

_____

59) Who was your favorite teacher(s) and what did they teach?

_____

_____

60) What were your most and least favorite subjects?

_____

_____

_____

61) What extra-curricular activities did you like to participate in?

_____

_____

_____

62) Who was your childhood arch-enemy?

_____

_____

63) What is the best gift you received? What was it and who gave it to you?

_____

_____

64) As a child, what did you want the most, but never got?

_____

_____

65) Do you have any memories of family gatherings or weddings?

_____

_____

66) What were your favorite cartoons and movies as a kid?

_____

_____

67) What was the first movie you watched at a cinema? Describe the film and the experience.

_____

_____

68) Did you have a favorite aunt, uncle or any other relative? Why?

_____

_____

_____

69) Where did your family go for vacations? Did you enjoy them?

_____

_____

70) How often did your family move when you were a child? And how did you feel about it?

_____

_____

_____

71) How many places have you lived in?

_____

72) Which house and neighborhood did you like living in the most?

Why?

_____

_____

73) Do you have any memories of your grandparents?

_____

_____

_____

74) Did your grandparents tell you any stories?

_____

_____

_____

Additional Notes

Teenage

"One of the cruelties of teenage-hood is that you'll never know what your parents were really like at your age, and they'll never accurately remember."

— Una LaMarche

75) How did you dress and do your hair in your teens?

_____

_____

76) What did you do as a teen that no one would do anymore?

_____

_____

_____

77) Where did you go to hang out with friends?

_____

_____

_____

78) How did you spend your weekends?

_____

_____

_____

79) Which activities made you nervous as a teenager?

_____

_____

_____

80) Which house chores did you have to do?

_____

_____

81) Which type of books did you read for fun?

_____

_____

_____

82) Who was your favorite author? Why?

_____

_____

_____

83) Which college did you attend?

_____

_____

84) What were your majors and how did you choose them?

_____

_____

_____

85) Did you like your college and teachers or not?

_____

_____

_____

86) Did you ever attend a boarding school or college? If so, how did you feel being away from family?

_____

_____

_____

87) Did you enjoy playing video games? How did you play them? Name some of your favorite ones.

_____

_____

_____

88) What were your special abilities in your teens?

_____

_____

_____

89) Did you try to make a music band with your friends?

_____

_____

_____

90) Did you want to be famous? If so, what for?

_____

_____

91) When and how did you learn to drive?

_____

_____

92) What was the first car you drove?

_____

93) What was your dream car?

_____

94) Who was your favorite musician or band?

_____

_____

95) Did you go to any concerts?

_____

_____

96) Which ones did you like the most? Why?

_____

_____

_____

97) Are you still in contact with any of your teenage friends?

_____

_____

_____

98) Did you unexpectedly meet any of them sometime later?

_____

_____

_____

99) Whom did you go to for advice? Why?

_____

_____

_____

100) Which party or event did you enjoy the most?

_____

_____

_____

_____

101) Which sports did you like? Why?

_____

_____

102) Who was your favorite player or athlete?

_____

103) Who was your mentor growing up? How did (s)he effect you?

_____

_____

_____

104) Were you a fan of a certain team?

_____

_____

105) When did you get a mobile phone?

_____

Did you ever do something dangerous as entertainment?

_____

_____

_____

_____

106) Did you attend a funeral of someone you were close to? How did you feel at their loss?

_____

_____

_____

Additional Notes

Adulthood

"Young people, when informed and empowered, when they realize, that what they do truly makes a difference, can indeed change the world."

— Jane Goodall

107) Which university did you go to?

_____

_____

108) What has been the most useful thing you learned in your formal education?

_____

_____

_____

109) How did you choose your career? Who or what influenced your choice?

_____

_____

_____

110) Are you satisfied with your career choice? If not, what would you change, if you had another chance?

_____

_____

111) Did you plan to get a job or start a business after completing your studies?

_____

_____

_____

112) Where and what was your first job or business?

_____

_____

_____

113) How old were you when you started working?

_____

_____

114) How did you working professionally for the first time?

_____

_____

_____

115) How much was your first pay or income?

_____

116) How did you spend it?

_____

_____

117) What is the most expensive thing you bought for yourself?

_____

_____

118) What is the most expensive gift you bought for someone else? Who did you give it to?

_____

_____

119) What was the most useful thing your parents have taught you?

_____

_____

_____

120) What is the best advice you have ever got?

_____

_____

_____

121) What is the best decision you've ever made?

_____

_____

_____

122) Which decision(s) do you regret the most? Why?

_____

_____

_____

123) What has been the proudest moment of your life?

_____

_____

_____

124) What do you think was the worst day of your life?

_____

_____

_____

125) What is the one life changing moment that changed your perspective or attitude?

_____

_____

_____

_____

_____

126) Have you ever won an award or distinction?

_____

_____

127) Have you ever met someone famous?

_____

_____

128) Has anyone ever broken your heart or trust?

_____

_____

_____

129) Have you ever been in a life threatening situation?

_____

_____

_____

_____

130) When did you feel proud of yourself?

_____

_____

_____

_____

131) Who has inspired you the most in your life? How?

_____

_____

_____

_____

132) Did you learn a foreign language? Where from?

_____

_____

_____

133) How did you meet my father?

_____

_____

_____

_____

134) What did you like about him the most?

_____

_____

_____

_____

135) What made you decide that you should marry him?

136) How long did you know each other before marriage?

137) When is your wedding anniversary?

Additional Notes

Motherhood

"Mothers give up so much, so that their children can have so much."

– Catherine Pulsifer

138) Did you like children, in general, before having your own?

_____

_____

139) Do you have any memories of a baby shower or an organized gender reveal party?

_____

_____

_____

_____

140) What was it like to become a mother for the first time?

_____

_____

_____

_____

141) What challenges did you face as a first-time mom? How did you overcome them?

_____

_____

_____

_____

142) Who was your go-to person when you needed parenting advice?

_____

_____

_____

143) What has been your biggest sacrifice for your children so far?

_____

_____

_____

144) How did you feel when I was born? What were your feelings when you held me in your arms for the first time?

145) How did you choose my name? Did you name me after someone? Why?

146) What was I like as a baby?

147) What were my siblings like as babies?

148) Did I ever annoy you big time?

149) What was the first birthday gift you gave me?

150) Was I obsessed with something you didn't want me to have?

151) What were my first words? What was your reaction to it?

152) Did I mispronounce any words that you found amusing?

153) Was I an easy-going child? Did I cry easily?

154) Was it hard to make me sleep?

155) What did you hate about me the most when I was a toddler?

156) What did you love about me the most when I was a toddler?

157) What did I call you as a toddler? How did you feel about it?

What was my reaction after the first day at school?

158) Were you a working mother or a home-maker? What did you prefer?

159) Is there anything about being a mom you wish you had known earlier?

_____

_____

160) As a mother, when did you have a very difficult time because of your children?

_____

_____

_____

161) Did your children quarrel frequently? How would you handle them if they did?

_____

_____

_____

162) What behavior of your children made you lose your temper with them?

_____

_____

163) Did you set any rules for your children? How did you penalize them if they broke them?

What is the cutest thing that I've ever done?

164) Have you made any parenting decisions that you would reconsider, if given another chance?

165)   Did your children turn out to be like you wanted them to be?

Did you ever feel helpless as a mother? How did you manage it?

Did you ever fear you would spoil your children? Why?

166) When did you have most fun with your children?

167) What was the nicest thing I have ever told you?

168) Did I ever embarrass you in front of relatives or in public?

169) Was there a family member you tried to keep your children away from? Why?

_____

_____

_____

170) What did you want me to become when I would grow up? Why?

_____

_____

_____

_____

171) In general, do you consider me a good child? Why? What about my siblings?

_____

_____

_____

_____

172) Have you ever taken part in social services? How was your experience?

_____

_____

_____

_____

173) Do you pray? If so, who do you pray to? Who or what do you pray for the most?

_____

_____

_____

_____

174) Do you give charity? If so, what makes you do it?

_____

_____

175) Did you ever suffer from financial problems? How did you get over them?

_____

_____

_____

_____

176) Did you have any character traits that you don't want me to have?

_____

_____

_____

177) Which celebrity are you a fan of right now? Why?

_____

_____

178) Do you have someone with whom you can share all your secrets?

_____

_____

_____

_____

179) If you could go back in time and change one thing, what would it be and why?

_____

_____

_____

_____

180) Which job did you enjoy doing the most? Why?

_____

_____

_____

_____

181) What are you most worried about?

_____

_____

_____

_____

182) What are you most thankful for in life? Why?

_____

_____

_____

_____

183) Which three people do you want to meet the most? Why?

_____

_____

_____

_____

_____

184) What are your biggest regrets in life?

_____

_____

_____

_____

185) How many countries have you been to? Which one is your favorite?

_____

_____

_____

_____

186) What is your favorite place and why? Have you ever been there?

_____

_____

_____

_____

187) What do you think were your best and worst investments?

_____

_____

_____

_____

188) What has been your favorite period of your life so far? Why?

_____

_____

_____

189) What do you wish you had wasted less time on? Why?

_____

_____

_____

190) What do you wish you had spent more time on? Why?

_____

_____

_____

_____

191) Which three events do you think shaped your life? How?

_____

_____

_____

_____

_____

192) Who are you most thankful to? Why?

_____

_____

_____

_____

193) Who has been the most interesting person you've met so far? Why do you think so?

_____

_____

_____

_____

194) How many life-time experiences have you had?

_____

_____

_____

_____

195) Did you have any health issues that you overcame?

_____

_____

_____

_____

196) What is the most valuable lesson you learned from a mistake? Describe the mistake and the lesson clearly as it would be valuable for me too.

_____

_____

_____

_____

_____

197) You've seen a huge enhancement in technology. Does life
seem simpler or more complicated now?

_____

_____

_____

_____

198) How do you want to be remembered by:

Your family:

_____

_____

Your children:

_____

_____

_____

Your friends:

_____

_____

Your colleagues:

_____

_____

People in general:

_____

_____

_____

_____

199) What do you think you are very good at?

_____

_____

_____

200) What do you think you are not so good at?

_____

_____

_____

201) How have your hobbies evolved from your childhood till now?

_____

_____

_____

202) What is the one thing that you want to overcome in yourself?

_____

_____

203) What do you think can be called 'the perks of being a mother'?

_____

_____

_____

_____

204) What do you think is the hardest thing about motherhood?

_____

_____

_____

_____

205) Have you ever had a strong argument with my father?

_____

_____

_____

_____

206) When did you two stand up for each other against someone?

---

207) What do you think people may not know about you?

---

208) What type of behavior always makes you angry? Why?

---

209) What is the nicest thing someone has ever done to you? How did you express your gratitude to them?

_____

_____

_____

_____

210) What is the nicest thing you have done for someone else?

_____

_____

_____

211) What does success mean to you? Do you think you have been or will be successful in life?

_____

_____

_____

_____

212) Did you have any fears that you struggled to overcome and succeeded?

_____

_____

_____

213) What creative stuff would you do only if you had enough time?

_____

_____

_____

_____

214) What qualities did you have at my age that you would like to see in me right now?

_____

_____

_____

215) Which three books would you recommend me to read? How would they benefit me?

_____

_____

_____

_____

_____

216) What three pieces of advice would you give me?

_____

_____

_____

_____

_____

_____

Additional Notes

Favorites

Who/What is your favorite:

Color

_____

Author

_____

Book

_____

Magazine

_____

Movie

_____

Actor

_____

Actress

_____

TV series

_____

Genre

_____

TV show

_____

Drama/Play

_____

TV channel

_____

Blogger / Youtuber

_____

Radio Station

_____

Song

_____

Artist

_____

Band

_____

Anchorperson

_____

Motivational speaker

_____

Quotation

_____

_____

Language

_____

City

_____

Leisure activity

_____

Holiday

_____

Shopping mall

_____

Vacation spot

_____

Sports

_____

Athlete

_____

Team

_____

Sports player

_____

Type of Food

_____

Dish

_____

Fruit

_____

Dessert

_____

Restaurant

_____

Car

_____

Car manufacturer

_____

Clothing and Fashion brand

_____

Animal

_____

Flower

_____

Perfume

_____

Flavor

_____

Drink

_____

Question in this book

_____

Additional Notes

_____

_____

_____

_____

_____

_____

_____

_____

_____

Emotions

The time you felt extremely:

Angry

_____

_____

_____

_____

Sad

_____

_____

_____

_____

Joyful / Happy

_____

_____

_____

_____

Anxious

Confused

Proud

Worried

_____

_____

_____

_____

_____

Shy

_____

_____

_____

_____

_____

Disappointed

_____

_____

_____

_____

_____

Excited

_____

_____

_____

_____

_____

Lonely

_____

_____

_____

_____

_____

Offended

_____

_____

_____

_____

_____

Fortunate

_____

_____

_____

_____

_____

Unfortunate

_____

_____

_____

_____

Disgusted

_____

_____

_____

_____

_____

Nervous

_____

_____

_____

_____

Hopeless

_____

_____

_____

_____

Overwhelmed

_____

_____

_____

_____

Hopeful

_____

_____

_____

_____

_____

Misfit

_____

_____

_____

_____

Describe:

Your father

_____

_____

_____

_____

Your mother

_____

_____

_____

_____

My father

_____

_____

_____

_____

Me

_____

_____

_____

_____

My siblings

_____

_____

_____

_____

Draw me something

Draw something. Anything, simple or complex, neat or rough.
Something meaningful, and deep, for me.

100

MOM

Thank You,

for filling it for me,

I'll try my best to make good use of it!

Made in the USA
Las Vegas, NV
30 November 2023